Sea-monster Soup

Written by Lisa Thompson

Pictures by Craig Smith and Lew Keilar

Captain Red Beard is hungry.

He wants his favorite food.

His favorite food is sea-monster soup.

First, he has to catch a sea monster.

Catching a sea monster is a very tricky job.

Sea monsters like to hide.

You need to trick the monster into coming out of hiding.

Captain Red Beard knows lots of tricks.

But what works one day may not work the next!

Sea monsters like special sounds.

Captain Red Beard makes sea-monster sounds into the water with a big horn.

Then he waits.

There is no sign of a sea monster.

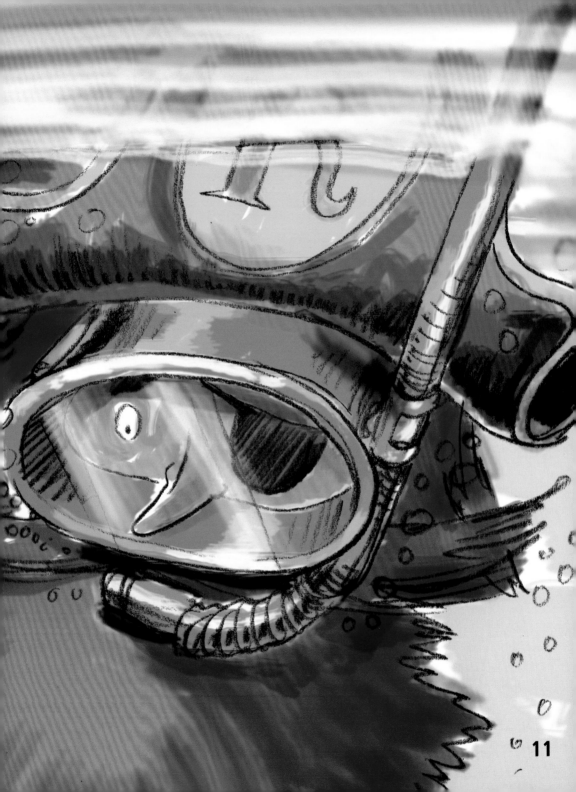

Sea monsters like special food.

He scatters sea-monster food into the sea.

Then he waits.

There is no sign of a sea monster.

fisherman's basket

13

Sea monsters love the color orange.

He sails the seas dragging a big orange net through the water.

Then he waits.

There is no sign of a sea monster.

Sea monsters like other sea monsters.

He makes a giant sea-monster balloon and ties it to his ship.

Then he waits.

There is no sign of another sea monster.

Captain Red Beard gives up.

He is too hungry to keep hunting sea monsters.

He has to eat something.

The only food left on the ship is
baked beans and bread.

The Captain makes baked beans on toast.

Now, there are sea monsters everywhere!

Sea monsters simply love baked
beans on toast.

24